Southern Kitchens & Dining Spaces

QUARRY

Design, Inspiration, and Hospitality from the American South

Southern Kitchens
& Dining Spaces

GLOUCESTER MASSACHUSETTS

QUARRY BOOKS

Alicia K. Clavell

First published in the United States of America by
Quarry Books, a member of
Quayside Publishing Group
33 Commercial Street
Gloucester, Massachusetts 01930-5089
Telephone: (978) 282-9590
Fax: (978) 283-2742
www.quarrybooks.com

Library of Congress Cataloging-in-Publication Data
Clavell, Alicia K.
    Southern kitchens and dining spaces: designs, inspiration, and
  hospitality from the American South / Alicia K. Clavell.
        p.   cm.
    ISBN 1-59253-327-2 (pbk.)
    1. Kitchens—Southern States. 2. Dining rooms—Southern
States. 3. Interior decoration—Southern States. 4.
Entertaining—Southern States. I. Title.
  NK2117.K5C54 2007
  747.7'970975—dc22

                                                    2006024826
                                                    CIP

ISBN-13: 978-1-59253-327-5
ISBN-10: 1-59253-327-2

10 9 8 7 6 5 4 3 2 1

Design: Michael Brock Design, www.mbrockdesign.com
Contributing writer: Laurel Saville
Cover image: Scot Zimmerman
Back jacket images: Mitch Hager/Courtesy of Harrison Design
Associates, (left); Emily Followill/Courtesy of Pineapple House
Interior Design, Inc., (middle, left); Scott Moore/Courtesy of
Pineapple House Interior Design, Inc. (middle, right); John
Umberger/Courtesy of Harrison Design Associates, (right)

Printed in China

CONTENTS

INTRODUCTION

THERE IS SOMETHING INHERENTLY EXCITING about cooking and entertaining that has nothing to do with the food. Many children discover this joy early with tea parties, toy kitchens, and plastic food and cookware. I first experienced the feeling at six years of age: My neighbor Molly and I perfected the art of making mud pies. All the other children agreed that our pies were the most extraordinary. Apparently, we had discovered just the right consistency of dirt to water that, when pushed flat and fine into pie tins, made for the perfect presentation. Though we were neither preparing nor eating real food, we were entertaining guests who came to share in the fun.

Later, in a kitchen outfitted with green linoleum and matching appliances, my mother and I made real pies from the crust up. She taught me her recipe for the perfect chocolate filling, demonstrated how to apply a fine layer of flour to the rolling pin, insisted I use only ice water to prepare the crust, and directed me to pinch the doughy edges just so. She helped me appreciate the joy of consuming a meal I had labored to prepare.

As an adult, I have longed to recreate the cooking adventures of my youth by combining the delights of entertaining and hospitality with good food. Now, far removed from my mother's kitchen and the mud hole of my childhood, I have created my own place to enjoy such experiences. And I'm constantly defining and redefining my own entertaining and cooking space. I imagine what I'd do with this wall or that—maybe I'll add window treatments, paint the cabinets, add new drawer pulls, or refinish the dining table. In putting together this book I found myself, as I hope you will, dreaming. The homeowners and design professionals featured here have allowed us to do just that—imagine the possibilities—by inviting us into their kitchens and dining spaces, into the heart of their homes, with unparalleled graciousness and true Southern hospitality.

Our featured homes span the South, from Flannery O'Connor's Georgia to Mark Twain's muddy Mississippi, from the shimmering Gulf Coast to the Texas hill country, and from sweet and sultry Louisiana to the breezy Carolina coast. These homes are situated down dusty country roads, in suburban cul-de-sacs, even in the lofts of cities now bursting at the seams with urban expansion. We've even featured a home or two outside the region but designed for relocated Southerners wishing to capture the spirit of a place they deeply love.

Because Southern style is as distinctive—and as varied—as the collection of states included in the region and the many personalities that populate them, this book includes a variety of decorating looks, including traditional, casual, rustic, eclectic, and modern. Is your décor sleek and minimalist? Do you incorporate the principles of feng shui, or are you a collector with groupings of beloved items that spill from every table? Do you prefer a rustic and hearty look or, perhaps, classic fine lines? Maybe your design personality just can't be defined. No matter. We've got interiors to inspire you.

But the South is too beautiful to keep you indoors. It's a playground for secret gardens, shaded courtyards, hardy climbing vines, and year-round blossoms. We'll whisk you away to al fresco rooms, kitchens, and dining areas just right for entertaining a houseful of unexpected guests, and to spaces perfect for an afternoon nap under the branches of a lofty shaded oak.

In this book we share not only a taste of the South's finest design and architecture, but also entertaining ideas, and decorating tips. Whether you're attempting to create a stellar centerpiece, looking for tabletop suggestions for your next impromptu gathering, or considering how to display an ever-growing collection of figurines, you'll find the answers here. Finally, our guide to kitchen and dining essentials will help you bring home the looks you love.

In the spirit of Southern hospitality, I raise a toast to good food, good friends, and the beautifully designed kitchen and dining spaces that house them both.

WHAT'S MY STYLE?

I HAVE AN APPRECIATION FOR ALL THE STYLES FEATURED IN THIS BOOK, BUT MY OWN HOME CAN ONLY BE DESCRIBED AS eclectic. A minimalist friend once looked around the space and declared, hand on hip, that no modernist could survive here. It's probably true. My living room is graced with slipcovered hand-me-down sofa and wingback chairs. The pillows are three Waverly prints that seem unrelated but work perfectly together. For a coffee table there's a grouping of three suitcases, and for a side table there's a set of upturned wine crates filled with antique letters and topped with glass. Above a painted chest is an old window frame turned into a photo gallery, and accessories include stacks of books on the floor and chairs where I've left drops and drips of candle wax to remind me of intimate gatherings and late-night talks.

In the kitchen and dining room, guests find more of the same. The dining room table is a fabulous 1950s retro red. Padded chairs sport upholstery-tacked buttons and slick seats. They offset the black and white checked tile and the clean white cabinetry of the adjoining kitchen. Collections abound, of course—pitchers, old photographs, old cookbooks.

If your own style is less easily discernable, we can help.

TRADITIONAL

YOU'RE A CLASSIC. FINE LINES AND HISTORICAL PERIOD furnishings pervade your space but you can appreciate tasteful new pieces that harken to another time. While you prefer both your wine and furnishings aged, you want the latest and greatest innovations in kitchen appliances. If you have hardwood floors, they are peppered with warm Oriental rugs, corners are filled with pieces placed at just the right angle to display favorite silver and fancy floral arrangements fresh from the garden. Your home is a showplace, your décor so tastefully done that if you don't volunteer to host the next ladies' luncheon or garden club gathering, someone is sure to do it for you.

You're multifaceted in your style, which can vary according to occasion. For example, your mountain cabin may be rustic and traditional and your beach house a blend of casual and traditional.

LEFT: *Hot pink marries winter white in this traditional space.*

RIGHT: *The designer uses furniture pieces to complement rather than compete with the Spanish architectural details throughout this room.*

RUSTIC

Patinas and paint, wood and warmth, are the defining factors in your home. Handmade accessories and antiques from grandparents grace the space. Furnishings are important, but sometimes less so than the views of nature's bounty just beyond your window. You are a nature enthusiast and an eco-friendly soul, and it shows. You're attracted to darker colors and bold, feel-good textiles and believe in a comfortable atmosphere. Friends and family who come to visit are sure to feel comfortable, cozy, and relaxed.

Leave it to you to find the most relaxed spot in any home. You play well with others, no matter their style.

ABOVE: *Whether it calls for an impromptu summer gathering or a hearty fall fling, rustic settings such as this are the perfect place for friends and family to gather. Here, a farmhouse table is set for buffet style entertaining. An elongated bench on one side is paired with rustic chairs on the other.*

CASUAL

Your design spaces are representative of the way you live—feet up on the tables, with textiles, including rugs and upholstery, comfortable and cozy. Leather seating, slipcovers, and elements such as limestone countertops that age gracefully with the house are perfect choices for your interior. Dinner parties are relaxed and frequent. Party clean-up consists of throwing the slipcovers in the wash and shaking out the rugs. Your style is fresh and shabby chic, but you don't lack sophistication. Friends, relatives, and gathering guests feel right at home; you may have a problem getting them to leave.

Ever the optimist, you'll get along well with every style—from rustic to modern.

RIGHT: *A grouping of perfectly placed seashells, candles and flowers fresh from the garden give the appearance that this gathering has been planned for two weeks instead of just two hours.*

MODERN

YOU'RE SLEEK AND STREAMLINED, URBAN AND COOL. YOU ARE the original urban outfitter. Everything has a place, and there's a place for everything. You may or may not have heard of the word feng shui, but your home makes it look like you have practiced the art for years before you understood the nuances of furniture arranging. Your furnishings and patterns have a Zen-like flow and your sleek sophistication is revealed in minimal lines and surfaces. But your home isn't all cold and stark sophistication, it's updated and cool—just like you.

Eclectic and casual styles are closet to your heart. Your style will clash with the rustic individual.

BELOW: A cubist would feel right a home with the geometric lines of this kitchen and breakfast area. Minimalist white cabinetry can make any space seem larger. A built-in art niche lends interest to the breakfast room, and a series of pendant lights lead the eye through the kitchen to discover similarly cool spaces beyond.

ECLECTIC

YOU HAVE THE SOUL OF AN ARTIST (MUCH LIKE JACKSON Pollock's, in particular) and you view a room as your canvas. Some may call you a packrat (an up-close and personal look in your closets, brimming with items large and small, reveals why), but you call it sentimentality. Simply put, you know what you love, and you don't mind holding onto it for a while, or longer. You love to mix and match and have a penchant for infusing a space with your personality. You have an innate ability to combine colors and furnishings that no one else would have deemed possible. An eighteenth-century farm table paired with modern leather chairs, displayed on a faux-fur rug? Why not? You can create aesthetic pairings no one would ever dream of.

Join your taste and talent with another eclectic, traditional, or casual designer, and it's a match made in heaven. While you can appreciate a modernist sensibility, you prefer to leave that sparse domain to others

RIGHT: This room serves to answer the age-old question— why can't we all just get along? Here, a traditional sideboard mixes with a hip round table, surrounded by casual dining chairs. Overhead, a chandelier with traditional and modern lines illuminates the eclectic look that pervades the space.

PART ONE
EXPLORING SOUTHERN STYLE

Q UILTERS AND NON-QUILTERS ALIKE CAN APPRECIATE THE AESTHETICS OF good patchwork. Varied shapes, patterns, and textures—pinstripes and polka dots, lace and linen—all carefully placed and held taut by a common thread. The South is like a quilt. The Southern landscape, we who live in it, and our ideas of style are as varied as the patches of a beloved homemade quilt, yet we're also bound by the common threads of our collective experience.

Our architectural and decorative heritage draws its influence from the Colonial, Federal, Greek Revival, and Romantic periods. Today those same traditions are translated into a wide array of looks ranging from the classic lines of traditional forms to the sleek spaces of modern design. Some people prefer a cozy and rustic ambience, and others desire a comforting casual mix. No matter what your style is, you'll likely relate to Southern author Willie Morris's observation that "in the South, perhaps more than any other region, we go back to our home in dreams and memories, hoping it remains what it was on a lazy, still summer's day twenty years ago."

Whether you are a homegrown Southerner, a newcomer to our region, or a displaced native who is able to return only for the holidays, may our style pages inspire you to create and treasure some of the South's best design.

TRADITIONAL

Writer and architectural maven Edith Wharton noted, "A classic is classic not because it conforms to certain structural rules, or fits certain definitions....It is classic because of a certain eternal and irrepressible freshness." Traditional or classic pieces—among them furnishings in the Chippendale, Queen Anne, and Georgian styles—are the indelible ink of our Southern past and the one in which much of our modern furniture is dipped. Their recognizable lines and charming detail never go out of style. Mixing and matching traditional architecture and furnishings creates a look that harkens to yesteryear. By paying attention to quality and proportion while giving a nod to the past, you can achieve a timeless design that translates to the future.

Interior designer Frank Randolph's designs are proof positive that traditional design doesn't mean stuffy or stodgy. In this room, distressed white chairs are paired with a mahogany table and set against a backdrop of creamy linens and apple green walls. But perhaps the look is best summed up by the classical column Randolph uses in a new way—as a pedestal on which to perch accessories.

INN STYLE

MARIANNE AND STEPHEN HARRISON, OWNERS OF THE RHETT House Inn, know a thing or two about creating a comfortable home environment. In fact, these Beaufort, South Carolina, inn owners pride themselves on anticipating the needs of guests and providing a comfortable retreat to retire to at the end of the day. Their guests were always happy, but the owners longed for a similarly welcoming retreat. They built one next to their inn. The home is new construction but is made to look old. They kept the décor simple, mingled the indoors and out, and splurged on creature comforts such as commercial-grade appliances for serious cooking. "He's the griller and prepares the turkey on holidays, but I really like to do most of the cooking," says Marianne. Though it's only a weeknight dinner and she's preparing for just the two of them, Marianne creates a gourmet meal of swordfish and scalloped potatoes that would make you ready to hop on the next plane to Beaufort.

These Beaufort, South Carolina, inn owners pride themselves on anticipating the needs of guests and providing a comfortable retreat to retire to at the end of the day.

INN THE KNOW

Inn owner Marianne Harrison offers tips on creating a comfortable retreat for your overnight guests. Follow her advice and guests will feel like they've splurged at a bed and breakfast. The only problem is that they may never want to leave.

Arrange orchids and fresh-cut flowers in every room.

Leave books and magazines for guests to read. For those with a penchant for penning, leave a journal or notebook for them to jot down their thoughts.

Keep the décor clean and simple, but surround yourself with favorite items.

Unless privacy is an issue, leave widows unfettered by treatments.

Leave fresh towels, soaps, shampoos, and lotions out for guests. Don't forget to top it all off with a robe and slippers.

LEFT: *An aged appeal was important in everything save the appliances. Commercial-grade appliances, such as the six-burner stainless-steel cook top, ensure cooking is a breeze.*

ABOVE: *Freshly squeezed lemonade, a sky-high pile of cookies, and crisp pressed linens are set out for homeowners or unexpected guests to enjoy. A freshly picked magnolia blossom is the perfect garnish.*

LEFT: *Creating inviting spaces is an art form, and these inn owners have certainly mastered it. On their porch, columns, moss hanging from the trees, and hanging baskets lush with fresh flowers provide a picturesque Southern setting that makes you want to step right in and while away the afternoon.*

ABOVE: *A sideboard is a convenient resting place to be used before serving afternoon refreshments on the veranda.*

TRADITION WITH A TWIST

ADISCERNING DESIGNER ONCE TOLD ME THAT IN ORDER TO BREAK the rules of design, you must first understand what those rules are. With the help of a savvy architect and designer, these Gillespie Coutny homeowners have done just that. They took traditional Texas design and gave it a twist. Classic arches, limestone building materials, and Old World–style furnishings take on a completely different look when infused with more modern Texas style.

"The intent was to respond to the regional vernacular architecture," says architect Don McDonald. "The owners were looking for an earthy rural kitchen as a counterpoint to their urban city existence," he says of this weekend getaway.

The large kitchen is the gathering place for the family, and it's literally located at the heart of the home. Don explains that this main structure, which houses the kitchen, is surrounded by three similar structures, or sheds. It's a throwback to the way families previously thought of home design—one main structure, with others added as needed. "The north shed contains the scullery and support for the kitchen. The south is a high-ceilinged screened porch that functions as an outdoor dining room next to the barbecue pit. The east shed, another porch with fireplace, is generally used as a cocktail area for before and after dinner," says Don of this multigenerational space.

Throughout, traditional details such as tidewater cypress, long-leaf pine, and Texas limestone mix and mingle and impeccably interact with modern touches such as raw polished concrete countertops.

LEFT: *Everything is bigger in Texas—the kitchens, the dining spaces, and certainly the views. If the limestone and exposed beams don't tip you off to this home's locale, one look out the window at the rolling hills lets you know you're in Texas hill country.*

RIGHT: *Traditional Texas materials mix with modern to yield a retreat that has an old-fashioned feel in an up-to-date context.*

CLASSIC STYLE

FRANK RANDOLPH GIVES NEW MEANING TO DOING THINGS THE old-fashioned way. He is traditional in the largest sense of the word, and it shows in both his designs and his life. He doesn't use cell phones—actually still has a land-line when some young folks don't remember what that is. "I'm a solo designer, and I need to have time for each individual. That means no email and no cell phone," affirms Frank. In fact, we conducted this interview the old-fashioned way by setting up an appointment and actually speaking. This is a novel approach in a world buzzing with new technology, but Frank's clients, particularly the owners of this home, appreciate this old-fashioned sentiment.

If you walked into this Georgetown kitchen twenty years from now, it would still be considered good design. "We painted the floors to look like old vintage," Frank says of the 24-inch (60 cm) black and white squares that cover the oak flooring. Ancient marble for the countertop and island is paired like a fine wine and choice cheese with clean white cabinetry and a subway tile backsplash.

"When you go into the dining room, you want it to be different," says Frank. And it is. Though these are sympathetic spaces, they are decidedly different. The table is set with crisp linens, fine china, and a fresh bouquet of hydrangeas. "But you're not walking into a stage set or over the top," says Frank. He points out that people would be comfortable dining here in casual clothing or black tie eveningwear. Frank may be old-fashioned when it comes to technology, but his designs span time and age.

If you walked into this Georgetown kitchen twenty years from now, it would still be considered good design.

LEFT: *It's almost as if the furnishings have placed a glamour spell on the eye. The verticle lines of a mirror above the mantel and a built-in niche draw the eye in and upward, making the this room seem larger than it is. The gentle curve of the armchairs is reflected in the extension of the crane's neck.*

FRANK'S TIPS ON SETTING A TRADITIONAL TABLE—WITH A TWIST

- "I think that most of all you want your space to be comfy and not too staged," says Frank.
- "There's no chandelier in here," notes Frank. Recessed lights and a pair of niches and candles are the only light in the room. After all, what Southern table is complete without candles? Frank recommends using 18- (46 cm) and 25-inch (63 cm) candlesticks, which are not too low and not too tall—just right.
- Keep centerpieces sophisticated and quiet. "People should shine as well as the food," says Frank.

ABOVE: *A white subway tile backsplash mixes with antique marble countertops and cabinetry that's both minimal and classic by design. A window above the sink brightens the space, and a single globe is lit when dusk descends.*

RIGHT: *The antique marbletop island and sink serves as both prep area and snacking space. In case you missed the striking French doors and beautiful view that beckons, the island seems to point the way to the breakfast room and the outside beyond.*

ABOVE: *A bevy of interesting table accessories work like a table runner—and, like other lines in the room, they serve to lead your eye in and through the space.*

RIGHT: *This serene space is indicative of many Frank Randolph designs. Without much rearrangement, he says, the space should accommodate both casual dinner gatherings and black-tie affairs.*

LOVINGLY RESTORED

SOME PEOPLE THINK NOTHING OF GATHERING IN THE FAMILY room to grab a quick bite in front of the television. But this Atlanta, Georgia, family takes both their dining and their restoration seriously. The home and dining room were lovingly restored with the help of Harrison Design Associates, but the entire family had a hand in it. The homeowner's son even researched original interiors down to (or up to, in this instance) the crown moldings. Furnishings and materials appropriate to the original structure grace the space, and now the family has a wonderful room in which to sit down and enjoy meals and each other.

The furnishings and accessories harken to the original look of the home. The table is set with linen and fine china in preparation for fine family dining. The baby blue color of the dining room is reminiscent of the ceiling color of Southern front porches. The color washes from the dining room into the party pantry.

Having these furnishings and materials appropriate to the original structure that grace the space ensures a place that preserves the charm and integrity of the home for years to come.

ABOVE: *Impromptu family entertaining? No problem. The adjoining butler's pantry has storage for dishes, crystal, napkins, and candlesticks.*

RIGHT: *Traditional homes, not unlike this one, shaded by giant oaks and tucked behind busy Atlanta, Georgia, streets provide respite from busy city life. This home, particularly the dining room, provides an epicenter for family life, worlds away from the cares of the city.*

THE BUTLER'S PANTRY

Traditionally, the butler's pantry was the place from which the butler staged dramatic dining; it also provided storage for all that wonderful Southern tableware. While many of us do not have a pantry with sink, countertop, and storage, many modern homes have variations on the butler's pantry—at least a cabinet or two designated for storage and a small closet for linens and dishes.

CLASSIC SUMMER HOME

LAKESIDE LIVING DOESN'T ALWAYS MEAN CASUAL BY DESIGN. THIS home, located on Georgia's Lake Oconee, offers regular casual comforts with the grand effect of a traditional Southern city home.

While some prefer their lake house in slipcovers, cheery or muted colors, and rustic beach furnishings, these homeowners chose a more traditional look. Bold colors and classic lines and materials harken to Southern yesteryear.

Views were integral in the design of this contemporary French cottage, explains Melissa Wilson of Harrison Design Associates. The classic furnishings are situated to take every advantage of the lake beyond. Myriad windows and doors catch summer breezes as well as scenery.

LEFT: *The breakfast room is set for casual dining by the lake. A pot of red tulips brightens the space.*

RIGHT: *An enclosed glass porch is the perfect transition from the kitchen and breakfast room to the lake beyond.*

ABOVE: *It's true that no matter where your party begins, guests will eventually gather in the kitchen. Luckily, this kitchen not only supports cooking but also offers tables and a large island to accommodate large gatherings.*

RIGHT: *This traditional city home has a touch of French country style. Case in point: "The large, custom-built ventilation hood bridges the space between the kitchen and the conservatory," says Melissa Wilson.*

RAISING THE BAR

SOUTHERNERS ARE FOND OF ENTERTAINING, SO THE TRADITIONAL Southern bar is a staple in many homes. The space has been made more efficient by incorporating bar and prep sinks, refrigerators, and even small dishwashers specially made for the bar area.

"The pass-through wet bar connects the library with the main flow of the house," says Melissa Wilson of Harrison Design Associates. The striking green walls and Verdi marble countertops make quite an impact in the already grand space.

RIGHT AND FAR RIGHT: *Arches have long been a staple of Southern design, and this built-in bar takes full advantage of such a fine architectural detail. The gentle arch overhead helps to soften the strong bold colors and necessary vertical and horizontal elements of the bar and adjoining library.*

TUDOR WITH A TWIST

THIS BIRMINGHAM, ALABAMA, HOME IS DECORATED WITH A NOD to its English Tudor roots, Tudor being the predominant style of the Redmont neighborhood in which it's built. Designer Mary Evelyn McKee followed that traditional look but infused the furnishings with what she calls a fresh twist.

"All the furnishings and fabrics were chosen with the historical reference in mind. We used a lot of linen prints, tweeds, and damasks," she says. The comfortable and beautiful furnishings, offset underfoot with Persian rugs, have proven successful for entertaining either "handfuls of friends or a large civic event."

LEFT: *Why take breakfast in bed when this built-in breakfast banquette is such a plump, cushiony place? Above the half-moon seating, traditional casement windows provide light and views of the surrounding neighborhood.*

RIGHT: *Neutrals work well when punctuated with pops of color. In this space, cool colors are emboldened with a striped silk antique settee. It provides the necessary color pop and also a spot to sit and reflect on the lovely ambiance of the room. A mirror situated above doubles the impact of the space.*

LEFT: *One look at this dining room gets you thinking about how to angle for a dinner invite. If dinner conversation wanes, remarks are sure to turn to the beautiful silver tablesetting and a dramatic centerpiece that's just the right height for guests to look over. French doors let in the light, but curtains can be pulled to for privacy.*

ABOVE: *This carved wooden chest sports two lamps to better illuminate the fine style of this dining room. The antique compote filled with fruits barely brushes the surface of the chest which is interchangeably used for storage and buffet style entertaining.*

BELOW: *Though there are many traditional elements in the kitchen, these barstools aren't among them. Three square stools provide stylish modern seating. They can be pushed up and underneath the classic island when not in use.*

CASUAL

SOUTHERNERS ARE GREAT CONVERSATIONALISTS, BUT SOMEtimes we like to let our home's interior speak for us. For example, casual design means "welcome home" in Dixie. Characterized by inviting interiors, including sink-in seating upholstered in soft, washable fabrics and coffee tables on which you can actually prop your feet, casual design means rooms you can actually live in. Whether you are a first-time visitor or a long-time friend, you will find that Southern casual instills an immediate sense of comfort and belonging. The homes in this section capture that welcoming feel without sacrificing style. You can almost hear them saying, "Come on in, y'all. Sit down and stay a while."

Homeowners and visitors alike can find casual comfort on this screened porch. French chairs and a table covered in a bright provincial cloth is a popular year-round gathering spot for people and for pets.

MAKING A SPLASH WITH COLOR

Homeowner Lisa Kelley jokes that it was her rebellious nature that inspired her colorful interiors. "My parents were builders, and for resale value we painted with neutrals," she says. Though she's tried the lighter side of paint, Lisa says bright colors speak to her. And, luckily, she listens.

Like many Southerners, Lisa looks to her environment to define her décor. She has painted her Boca Raton, Florida, home in bougainvillea, coral, lemon, and Key lime. Orange and russet hues brush against brilliant blues, and the red and green tones of tropical foliage flourish on her walls. The entry gently ushers guests into a home where a vibrant color awaits at each turn. In the kitchen, cabinets are painted sage green, and sunny yellow walls reflect the disposition visitors are bound to adopt after even the briefest stay. In the dining room, bright bougainvillea accentuates the warm wooden table, and a crisp white service piece virtually pops against one wall.

But paint is only part of designing a fun, functional space. This mother of four achieves attractive yet livable interiors simply by channeling her innate sense of style into how her beach-loving family lives. She creates a stylish balance by pairing punches of tropical color with comfortable furnishings.

With four kids, she must be prepared for extra guests at all times. Cooking and entertaining on the fly mean no-fuss table decorations are must-haves. Grouping collections of vases and seashells offers dramatic impact.

This mother of four achieves attractive yet livable interiors simply by channeling her innate sense of style into decorating for how her beach-loving family lives.

LEFT: *A chandelier embellished with seashells illuminates no-fuss table decorations such as the shell-filled glass vase. Create your own centerpiece using clear vases and shells that have been thoroughly cleaned. Tuck in tall sea grass or reeds for height and color.*

RIGHT: *This home is a playground for the eye and a feast for the senses. A surprising rainbow of tropical color ushers visitors from the foyer into the kitchen where painted cabinetry is only one of the bright spots. Beyond the kitchen is the patio, pool, and garden, where it's clear the homeowner drew her color inspiration.*

LEFT: *The casual elegance of Lisa's Boca Raton, Florida, home literally spills out and into her backyard. This is one venue where every seat in the house is a good one. Guests can pick from several posh poolside spots to view a friendly game of sharks and minnows. The porch overhang provides some respite from the summer sun, but most guests eventually succumb to the promising pull of a gazebo just beyond.*

RIGHT: *This outdoor gazebo is a favorite spot of homeowners and guests alike. A multitude of comfortable chairs, including painted benches and tufted, pillowed rockers, makes for a great place to relax. When teamed with Boca breezes and music from the lazy canal just below, it's hard to resist the sandman's call. The roof guarantees no one will wake up burned.*

LEFT: *This outdoor drop zone serves many of the same functions as an indoor mudroom. There's no need to drip dry when you can just as easily grab a fresh towel, robe, or hat from one of the decorative wire hangers. Once dry, guests can pull up to one of the pretty pink wicker stools to refill a drink or don a pair of flip-flops from a nearby bench.*

RIGHT: *White slatted furniture is good looking and easy to maintain. Black and white striped cushions add a bold pattern to the minimalist white slatted furniture. Here and there, towels are tucked into baskets, and hats and sunglasses are readily available to ensure that friends, family, and unexpected visitors are comfortable.*

BRINGING THE PARTY OUTSIDE

THE REGION'S MILD CLIMATE MEANS THAT MANY GATHERINGS that begin indoors end under starry Southern skies. It's no wonder that Southerners looking for the idyllic getaway need search no farther than their own backyard. The weather allows for indoor/outdoor spaces such as kitchens, decks, sunrooms, courtyards, patios, and, of course, porches.

In this al fresco space, for example, views of the sur-rounding country, cooling breezes, and the promise of good food entice guests. In fact, this Austin, Texas, outdoor kitchen and dining space, fitted with a built-in grill and comfortable seating area, often receives more attention than its interior counterparts. Whether you're serving an impromptu lunch-eon or a formal dinner, this area promises the meal will move at a relaxed pace, allowing plenty of time to visit.

It's no wonder that many
Southerners looking for the idyllic getaway need search
no further than their own backyard.

LEFT: *The built-in grill is offset by surrounding stone and gentle arches that echo the exterior architecture of the home. The nearby table offers dining space that will stand up to the heat and humidity of the climate.*

ABOVE: *The outdoor cooking space is convenient to the kitchen making preparation and serving a breeze. The wood tones of the door moldings blend with the detail of the exterior porch.*

THE SIMPLE LIFE

SIMPLICITY REINS SUPREME IN THIS VERO BEACH, FLORIDA, home. Nowhere is that more evident than in the dining room and adjoining courtyard. Architect Tom Payette created his home away from home using varied wood tones and a soothing palette of white and cream. High-set windows, unfettered by treatments, allow for ample light and draw attention to the expansive ceiling. During the day, rays of light flit about the room, making patterned prisms that dance intermittently on the walls, floor, and ceiling. Once the sun ducks low in the horizon, guests bask in the glow of man-made orbs—two chandeliers that hang low and full. French doors open onto a patio where statuesque columns line up like party guests and vines send tendrils along stucco walls. The background music of crashing waves is piped in on the breeze, and the grandfather clock in the adjoining room keeps a peaceful pace, noting the minutes, hours, and days lost in this serene space. It is the only one keeping real time at this serene beach retreat.

ABOVE: *A shaded overhang allows guests to retreat from the sun while still enjoying the day. Beach music breezes and plump pillows help guests forget their cares.*

RIGHT: *Wash-and-wear slipcovers such as the ones on the chairs surrounding this elongated table are a must-have at any beach property. Dress up slipcovers with embellishments such as ribbons and monograms.*

DESTINATION HOME

THIS AUSTIN, TEXAS, COUPLE SEARCHED FOR A NEW HOME to meet the needs of their growing family, but they ended up where they had started. When they couldn't find a space they loved as much as the one they were already in, they decided to remodel. Luckily, owner Michael Antenora knew a good architect—himself. He and his wife expanded the existing kitchen and dining room and created a seamless blend of interior and exterior courtyard spaces. Now the couple can make and break their bread without bumping elbows, and their children, friends, and family have plenty of room in which to visit and play.

The home's design is Southern, but with a Japanese twist. "The house was designed around the courtyards and around the physical and visual interplay of interior spaces and exterior courtyards," notes Michael. "This concept of seeing the destination, but with no direct path to get there, is endemic to traditional Japanese architecture." In many ways, the same concept led them to once again make their house their home.

> *"This concept of seeing the destination, but with no direct path to get there, is endemic to traditional Japanese architecture."*
>
> —architect and homeowner, Michael Antenora

Michael Antenora on blending Southern California, Japanese, and Texas style

"I've studied the traditional wooden, clay tile and rice paper Japanese home. I'm also very fond of the Arts and Crafts style, especially in its Southern Californian expression, and discovered that it was influenced by the design of Japanese houses. When we began remodeling, I noticed that the house already had a bungalow scale and proportion. So, I broke the house down into simple shapes put together in a complex way, just as traditional Japanese homes are based on the proportion of tatami mats. Another element is the deep eaves, found in both Craftsmen and Japanese styles. Because Texas is hot and people spend a lot of time outdoors, the eaves provide shade and look good doing it. Our house is also planned around the idea of seeing a place without having a direct route there—you can sit in the breakfast area and look through galleria into the master bedroom, or sit in dining room and look across breezeway into the soft courtyard. This reflects the Shinto philosophy that the path of life is not direct, but the destination is worthwhile."

RIGHT: *The kitchen is lined with light-colored cabinetry that provides plenty of storage space, including open shelving for assorted pots. Both modern and traditional fixtures have their place, and an open area just beyond leads to the breakfast room.*

LEFT: *Sometimes it takes a second go-around to get it right. This remodeled kitchen features upgraded appliances and copious new storage space.*

RIGHT: *The family often takes their meals in the adjacent hard courtyard, which affords lovely Austin views.*

DRESSY CASUAL

THIS ATLANTA, GEORGIA HOMEOWNER SPENT YEARS COLLECTING decorative and architectural elements from her travels abroad. Jenny Papevies didn't know how or when, but she knew her treasures—tiles, architectural pieces, and other odds and ends—would eventually be put to good use. When the opportunity arose to work with a group of talented individuals on a makeover for a magazine, she jumped at the chance to realize her dream kitchen. In the end, the kitchen came together much like a jigsaw puzzle—preservation, creativity, and a little bit of adhesive in just the right spots guaranteed the pieces would fit together perfectly.

Jenny's home, particularly her kitchen and dining room, is filled with custom touches, including the new maple kitchen cabinets that were aged by hand. The homeowner distressed them with chains and nails, and then added a glaze to give an Old World feel. The walls, too, were ragged with an umber glaze for depth and dimension. And that furniture piece isn't an armoire; it's a refrigerator in disguise. There's no junk in the trunk either—dog food and dog bowls are hidden in there. It can be opened at feeding time and then closed to clear the clutter. Salvaged architectural corbels were used in several spots, including on the island, over the stove, and on the fridge.

LEFT: *Collections of majolica and aged green tiles complement the aged wood tones in this new kitchen that is made to look old.*

RIGHT: *Not everything is as it appears in this space. The refrigerator is made to look like a built-in armoire, and the trunk in the corner is connected to the wall and holds dog bowls and dog food.*

LEFT: *Countertops, cabinetry, and other elements of the kitchen have been aged to reflect the Old World ambience the homeowner sought.*

ABOVE: *This Atlanta homeowner's dining area, located just off the kitchen, opens to the outdoors and allows cooling breezes to enter.*

CASUAL IN KEY WEST

THE STORY GOES THAT KEY WEST, FLORIDA, ONCE CONSIDERED the richest city in the United States, built its wealth on salvaging wrecked ships. One designer and real estate agent found a bounty all his own when he happened upon this turn-of-the-century home, built by a ship's captain. Like ship captains of yore, he salvaged materials and then put them to good use as treasures in his own home.

"I tried to keep it nautical," says homeowner Trip Hoffman of his own design schematic. But you won't find life preservers, oars, or other typical seafaring memorabilia. What you will find is a home that's in shipshape condition—neat and nautical in its minimalist nature.

Palm Meadow, as it's dubbed, features rooms painted in colors of Key West—a slight seaspray hue and a delicate seafoam green wash over every path and then lightly recede, leaving treasures in their wake. Here and there, antiques mix with found objects such as yard-sale chairs. Pairs of balustrades are made into a table, and salvaged wood is used for kitchen cabinets.

Trip says he follows the good weather, and his house seems to follow the same thought. Outside is a covered loggia with an elongated table. Inside, a wonderful table with wonderful apple green and bright white sets the pace. Both are equally enjoyable and follow the throng of the crowd in this fair-weather house.

Trip says he follows the good weather,
and his house seems to follow the same thought.

Trip Hoffman on salvage operations

"In Key West, homes like this belonged to ship-wreckers, who'd lure ships onto the reef and lay claim to everything. They called themselves salvagers. Some of the moldings and the kitchen cupboards were milled from Dade County pine left over from the restoration. It's a hardwood, the only thing in the tropics that termites won't eat, and it's now extinct. The dining room table is mid-1800s, from the very first bank ever in Key West. The legs on the table in the loggia are balustrades from the original convent and girl's school, salvaged from their porch. Also the home contains a lot of things from the original Key West lighthouse. We spend part of each year in Michigan, North Carolina, Key West, and Puerto Rico, and I just hunt stuff from antique stores, flea markets, and yard sales. I also buy historic houses and renovate them. As things are changed, I might salvage something for another house. I have an eclectic style, but to avoid a cluttered look, I recommend you decide on just a few colors repeated throughout, keep collections together and assimilated, and focus on certain forms, shape, and space, with an emphasis on space."

RIGHT: *A crisp white table and plump pillows are a welcoming contrast to the heat of a Key West summer day. Trip had this table made from old balustrades. Curtains can be pulled for shade and privacy.*

Paint Pointers

"Paint can change the whole scope of things," says Trip. Here, he shares some of his painting pointers:

- Painting just one wall in a room can change the entire look and feel of the space.
- Don't be afraid to try a new finish. Wooden mahogany chairs in Trip's dining room were stressed and distressed in blue, brown, white, and then green. Then they were sanded to let each color seep through.
- Keep things simple; don't overdo. Trip recommends working with an easy color palette—nothing formal or serious.
- Trip suggests choosing one or two colors to decorate your space. It's amazing how different the same colors can look in different light and at different angles. "I just finished a lake house in North Carolina. I chose only three colors and worked them throughout and mixed in great fabrics," he says.

LEFT: *Trip always has an eye out for salvaged materials and incorporates them with his interior designs. He built this corner cabinet from salvaged windows he found in North Carolina.*

ABOVE: *This table came from the original bank on Key West. Surrounding chairs are yard-sale finds painted in several colors and stressed to let the varied hues show through.*

ABOVE: *"It was a difficult house to furnish because of the natural pine colored walls,"* says Trip. *All the cabinetry was salvaged from Dade County pine and custom milled to fit the space.*

RIGHT: *A teak buffet with iron grilles enhances one end of the dining room. Green fabric behind the grilles brings out the color of the walls. And if the waves and beach music outside don't remind you you're in the Keys, the piece is topped with two vases and a bowl of seashells.*

ABOVE AND LEFT: *Gentle arched French doors, exposed beams, and tile floor combine Old World Italy with Southern sensibility. Sunlight floods the space. An elongated table provides a place for guests to gather and sample while the cooks put on a show nearby.*

RIGHT: *New appliances are housed in Old World cabinetry. The wood tones and muted colors reflect hand-hewn workmanship*

SOUTHERN ITALY

SOUTHERNERS AND ITALIANS HAVE A LOT IN COMMON. BOTH have a penchant for combining sophisticated grace and style with casualness. And in both groups, when good friends and family gather, the meal can go on and on, lasting well into the night. So what happens when Southern and Italian sensibilities meet? One architect and homeowner found out when he combined the two in this big city retreat.

The architect lives and works in the bustle of Atlanta, Georgia, and at the end of the day he needs—as so many of us do—a serene retreat, beautiful, but a place where friends and family could gather in unparalleled style.

Melissa Wilson of Harrison Design Associates points out some of the traditional Tuscan finishes, including white plaster walls, reclaimed white oak beams, and a floor made of antique terra cotta tile. "Natural materials are essential to the image of Italy, and here tall arched doors are made of cherry and kitchen cabinets are fashioned from maple," she says. The grand arches and casual eating spaces of the kitchen illustrate this duality of design.

ABOVE: *Light green window treatments complement the subtle tones. They can be left open to let in the light or pulled to for intimate gatherings.*

RIGHT: *In the dining room, elegant chairs embroidered with the homeowner's initial make a bold statement.*

It wouldn't take much to imagine that one was in Tuscany instead of the gentle rolling hills of Atlanta.

LEFT: *When it gets too hot in the kitchen, guests can cool off on the loggia just outside. Gentle architectural arches mimic the arched doors inside.*

ABOVE: *Dinner can be topped off with gelato at the farmhouse table. A fireplace and an open bottle of vino keeps guests warm on chilly Southern nights.*

RUSTIC

Long ago, the Earth was formed, and our landscape was birthed at a slow Southern pace. Ambling bedrock molded itself into peaks and valleys, mountains that we know today as the Appalachians and Great Smokies. Somewhere a seed sprouted, multiplied, and soon trees danced up and down the sweet mountain curves, blanketing everything in a green sea that shed and shimmered to gold and red in the cooler months.

For generations, we Southerners have drawn influences from these mountains and the soothing music created by the rustling wind through the leaves and the gurgle of water splashing over rocks made smooth by time. We scoop this earth into pottery, carve bowls from the grand hardwood trees of our forests, and create eclectic twig furniture from the vines that tangle through the region. We bring these things into our homes, pairing the best of cozy rustic design with the latest modern conveniences to yield a relaxed comfortable style that exudes Southern hospitality.

RIGHT: *Exterior elements like wood, stone, plant materials, and an animal hide bring the outdoors into this rustic room.*

RUSTIC RETREAT

RYAN GAINEY'S ATLANTA, GEORGIA, GUEST HOME READS LIKE A tactile family album: here an iron teakettle from his grandmother, there antique salt and pepper shakers, treasured photos, and other family heirlooms. Handmade furnishings pair with treasured family influences. In the dining room, a grand antler chandelier serves as a focal point. The handmade table is crafted from 200-year-old heart pine floors, and the chairs and other furniture are made from tin and wood. Silver accessories provide the perfect accent in this comfortable atmosphere. "Silver reminds me of the goddess Artemis, a Greek moon goddess," says Ryan.

The kitchen continues the rustic theme. The refrigerator hides behind a floor-to-ceiling cabinet. The counter is uncluttered by microwaves or other appliances. Modern conveniences need not be hidden because they aren't there. "I make everything by hand," says Ryan with pride.

In every room, potted plants or flowers brighten tables, corners, and windowboxes. "When people use the word rustic, they think of rust and old windows and Shabby Chic. I am not Shabby Chic," Ryan says emphatically. His home offers a rustic Southern charm that transcends the stereotype.

Charm School

Ryan Gainey shares his tips on achieving Southern charm:

- "Look to your family for inspiration," says Ryan, who surrounds himself with treasures from family members. "When people walk in my home they experience the history of my life."

- Plants can enliven spaces and fill in gaps, making a space feel more cozy. Practically every room, every corner of Ryan's guest house, and every table has a growing plant. "I even have two from my great-grandmother's garden," says Ryan.

- Everything looks better by candlelight, even Ryan's already lovely dining room. Use candles for gracious ambience at your next dinner party or soirée.

LEFT: *Wood furniture and warm touches make this city house feel as if it's located in the mountains. In the dining room, the antler chandelier serves as focal point and makes for interesting dinner conversation.*

ABOVE: *A farm sink with pedestal feet does homage to the old days and speaks of the way Ryan likes to do everything— the old-fashioned way.*

ABOVE: *In this backyard guest retreat, friends and family can bask in the warm glow of friendship and togetherness. Ryan uses candles for a festive glow at every gathering. Classic white candles, including tea lights, votives, and candlesticks tucked into greenery, grace the space. You can never have too many candles.*

RIGHT: *Ryan sets the table with a mixture of beautiful tableware and plants. This designer and landscaper has his hand in everything. He even has his own line of tableware, now available at www.abigails.net.*

LEFT: *How does your garden grow? Ryan's outdoor spaces are just as wonderful, if not more so, than his interior designs. This table, hidden beneath branches that drape like soft window treatments, offers quiet shade, conversation, and a view of the surrounding gardens.*

ABOVE: *Walls with patinas of gold and green bridge the gap between the wonderful garden space and the interior guest retreat.*

LOVE THAT RED

FEW FOLKS KNOW HOW TO ADD SEASONING LIKE THOSE IN Cajun country, so it's not surprising that this spicy red kitchen belongs to Louisiana homeowners. Though Pat and Jack Holden could have chosen any color under the sun, these design-savvy homeowners painted their cabinetry fire engine red. Cabinets are inset with fabric panels and feature baskets instead of closed-face drawers to hold silverware, napkins, and other kitchen accessories.

Chenal, Louisiana, residents Pat and her husband are experts on Louisiana furniture, crafts, and textiles, and that's obvious from a tour of their house, especially the kitchen. Their collection isn't one to be put in stuffy display cases; these antiques and collectibles beg to be touched, held, and told stories about.

From floor to ceiling, there's something interesting to look at. Above, exposed ceiling rafters draw the eye up to a collection of ceramic jugs and jars. Below, warm and yawning floorboards are covered in handwoven rugs. They draw interest and call out for bare feet. Louisiana treasures abound: handwoven baskets, paintings by local artists surrounded by handmade wooden frames, and punched tin panels inset into the bright red cabinetry. Have a seat in one of the many rocking chairs and stay a while to enjoy the down-home feel.

These antiques and collectibles beg to be touched, held, and told stories about.

Pat Holden on Acadian culture

For over forty years, we've been interested in the material culture of the late eighteenth- and early nineteenth-century Louisiana, with a focus on the French attitude, especially the Acadians who came down from Nova Scotia. The culture was conservative in that it didn't change much and the Acadians maintained many of their traditions, such as spinning and weaving fabrics for clothing as well as household bedding. They also liked to paint their furniture, and they used a red iron oxide pigment for barns and architectural elements. We could buy that pigment here up until the 1960s, because it was still favored. They also used Paris green for shutters and trim, which gets its color from copper acetoarsenite and is used as a pigment and wood preservative. We are interested in preserving vernacular houses, the auxiliary buildings that are not grand but rather were lived in by regular people. This building was threatened with oblivion, so we brought it to our grounds and restored it as a guesthouse for friends and family. We also had a family of Hurricane Katrina victims living there. This kitchen is modernized and put inside the house, which was historically rare, as kitchens were separated because of the heat and chance of fire.

RIGHT: *Open baskets are perfect for storing everything from napkins to silverware, and they keep everything within easy reach. They're more rustic than closed-drawer fronts and work as a nice juxtaposition to the Louisiana style fabric panels, which allow for air circulation.*

LEFT: *Even though it's hidden, you can't miss this bright red kitchen just off the rear entry. Wood tones and handmade crafts offset the brilliant red. Jack and Pat explain that the color was inspired by a common earth pigment, brun d'Espagnol or gros rouge, as it's called in Cajun country. "It is a natural iron oxide and varies in color depending on the source, but it is usually a reddish brown," says Jack.*

ABOVE: *You can put a story to almost every pitcher and jug in this collection. Jack Holden explains that rum was the favored beverage in Louisiana and that it was dispensed in reusable jugs like these. "The jugs on display were used in this area and are labeled with local distributors' marks," says Jack. He found shards of them around the house as well.*

TENNESSEE BRILLIANCE

IN THE FALL, TENNESSEE HIGHWAYS AND BYWAYS BURN WITH brilliance almost as bright as the hopes of a young country singer just arrived in Nashville. The leaves of the trees shed from green and to gold and back again, leaving seasons in their wake. Brentwood homeowners Larry and Carol Atema draw their inspiration from these mountains and have dressed their dining room in the brilliant colors of the Tennessee Valley—just when fall color is at its peak.

Russet tones, golds, and sweet clementine hues grace the space. Warm wood furnishings show well-loved wear. Underneath, a warm rug weaves the colors of the room together and encourages guests to slip out of dinner shoes and settle in for the evening. A fireplace adds welcome warmth to the space on those cool nights, and a simple wooden mantel displays plates, fall foliage, or whatever seasonal whim inspires. The mantel mimics the wooden doorframes, above which are displayed silvered plates that reflect the casual, cozy ambience.

Brentwood homeowners Larry and Carol Atema draw their inspiration from the mountains and have dressed their dining room in the brilliant colors of the Tennessee Valley —just when fall color is at its peak.

Larry Atema on using old and new elements in restoration

The room is actually an original Tennessee log cabin from 1796, contained within several additions to the house. Working with advice from the Colonial Williamsburg Foundation, we used materials, fabrics, and collections that were accurate to the era. Because this breakfast room is next to a formal dining room, we tried to keep it upscale while maintaining some casual elements. The curtains are period fabric lined with a blue and white check; the plates are good, old pewter; and the rug has a primitive geometric design that is both formal and fun. The plank table and Windsor chairs are reproductions of period pieces. The brick at the top of the fireplace is new, while the stone at the bottom is original to the cabin. When we started the restoration, we didn't even know the logs were there. We peeled back the entire two-hundred-year history of wall finishes, from knotty pine through plywood, leather, rough hides, and newspapers, and eventually we found the logs.

LEFT: *If furnishings could sing, these would surely belt out something country—perhaps a beautiful ballad similar to the ones the homeowners enjoy while preparing a hearty breakfast or dinner in their Tennessee dining space.*

OLD KENTUCKY HOME

Hang your derby hat at the door, and come on in for a drink. If the bourbon doesn't warm you, it's certain that the comfortable mix of rustic and astute finds will.

Classic Kentucky furnishings and accessories abound in this dining room. Antique high chairs and colorful glass decanters that probably once held good Kentucky bourbon balance the buffet. Around the table, ticking-fabric cushions are tied onto ladderback chairs to keep guests comfy. Above the dining room sideboard, a lovely scene depicts the Kentucky wilds, and a sterling silver mirror doubles the brilliance.

These owners think of the mantel like any furniture piece in the home and decorate accordingly. It provides a wonderful venue for displaying designs. Above one fireplace is a grouping of dried flowers and a mortar and pestle. A spinning wheel sits in one corner; handmade candles are on display in another. Above the other fireplace, sterling candlesticks topped with hand-dipped candles are surrounded by glass. They can be lit for those parties that are sure to last long into the Southern night.

"We will sing one song for the old Kentucky home
For the old Kentucky home far away."

—chorus from the Kentucky state song, *My Old Kentucky Home*

LEFT: *Atop this antique sideboard a silver tea setting is flanked on either side by hurricane lanterns. The wall mural has depth and integrity and offers a spectacular backdrop for the warm and inviting setting.*

RIGHT: *The owners use their home to display collectibles and treasures, like these beautiful glass decanters.*

LEFT: *This hand-painted mantel is a brilliant focal point. Above it, the owners display found treasures such as antique lanterns. A gilded mirror gives double the showy display.*

ABOVE: *Dried tufts of Kentucky wildflowers grace the space above the mantel in this dining room.*

Magic with Mantels

Treat your mantel to a makeover with these easy tips:

- Change your mantel décor with the season or at whim. An easy way to is fill vases with showy fresh or dried flowers according to the season.

- Think balance and symmetry. If you add a vase to one side of your mantel, balance it with a second on the other side. This doubles the impact while maintaining simplicity of design.

- To add horizontal lines and height, place a mirror or piece of art above the mantel. If you're considering art, check with a local gallery to ensure the fireplace heat won't damage your piece.

SWEET HOME ALABAMA

EVEN THOSE LUCKY ENOUGH TO LIVE NEAR OUR COOL waters and dip a toe in the Gulf any time it suits sometimes feel the need to flee to higher and cooler elevations when summer heats up. When it gets too hot in their home city of Birmingham, Alabama, the Weinheimers retreat to their cool Mentone, Alabama, cabin.

The owners decorated their cabin, especially the kitchen and dining space, with simplicity and style. The unobtrusive cozy and comfy furnishings make it hard to miss the striking green kitchen cabinets. The less colorful dining room opens to a wraparound porch where the brilliant cabinets are all but forgotten with the mountains' showy display of green, red, and gold. Patinas of peeling paint, dried flowers, and favorite antique jugs abound. The remainder of the home, particularly the porch, is peppered with rustic twig furniture. Visitors can't resist pulling up a chair and breathing in the glorious view of this—their sweet home, Alabama.

LEFT: *Bright green cabinetry is striking against the less showy wood tones of the furnishings.*

ABOVE: *An elongated wooden table is perfect for entertaining friends and family. Even during a large dinner party, the sing-song breezes and the mountain air enjoyed on the porch make it hard to notice anything else.*

ECLECTIC

WHAT SETS THE FINEST CHEFS APART IS THEIR ABILITY to combine unexpected ingredients in a single brilliant dish. Eclectic design requires the same sort of creativity. In the right hands, dashes of this design and pinches of that can result in something new and surprisingly attractive. To get this look at your home, mix modest with modern, pair something old with something new, or combine patinas and paint with the sleek and sophisticated. Break boundaries, bridge styles—and, above all, have fun.

The designer used sleek, chrome barstools and a slim chrome table to maximize open space in this small breakfast nook. To see more of this West Palm Beach home, turn to page 114.

A MODERN CLASSIC

"I BELIEVE THAT COLOR, BE IT WHITE OR GREEN, IS IMPORTANT," says Austin, Texas, designer Vickee Byrum. It is no surprise that someone with a design firm named Yellow Door Design loves vibrant hues. In the homes Vickee decorates, color starts at the entry and then, in a wavelike motion, spills, tumbles, and falls into room after room. The inspiration behind this particular color splash was a Tiffany jewelry box. "At first, everyone, including the painters, thought I was crazy," Vickee remembers. Now, even the practical painters agree that the blue is best.

The vivid color choice showcases the interesting combination of furnishings. "I love mixing designs from two time periods," says Vickee. In this dining room, for example, a traditional Stickley table is paired with funky acrylic chairs modeled after a Louis XVI design. Like many pieces in the home, the chairs are modern in style but classic in form. In the center of the table, a pair of vases sports bountiful bouquets. The vases are sometimes changed out for a makeshift table runner of colorful pottery borrowed from the kitchen. Vickee suggests adding interest to your own home by frequently rotating table displays. She says you can't go wrong with a colorful classic like gerbera daisies.

In the homes Vickee decorates, color starts at the entry and then, in a wavelike motion, spills, tumbles, and falls into room after room.

Vickee Byrum on making big use of a small space

This was a second home, and the client needed to be able to live in it with just two adults and two dogs or with her extended family over Thanksgiving. It's small, only 1,700 square feet (159 square meters) over three floors, so placement was key. The pantry is on the easiest path to get into and out of the kitchen, to feed the animals or grab a cereal box. The island is fat and wide so two people can sit there comfortably, or it's a place to put appetizers and act as a buffet for a bigger group. The island also contains the junk drawer, the microwave, and shelves for mixing bowls, so it's anything but empty space. All the drawers were designed specifically for what's in them; there's one for baking, one for water bottles, one for spices and herbs. And the color is just fun and playful and embraces the client's personality. Plus, it distracts from the fact that the space is so small because you don't think about it. You just walk in and think, "Wow, this is so amazingly cool."

LEFT: *The vivid wall color, inspired by a jewelry box, allows other elements, including exposed timbers and classic white marble countertops, to shine.*

ABOVE: *This kitchen is a little bit country and a little bit rock-and-roll. Slick stainless-steel appliances and stark white marble pop against the bright blue walls. Down-home heart cabinet pulls mix and mingle with sleeker elongated ones on other cabinets. Small sheers cover the window and let the light play over the eclectic look.*

RIGHT: *"Pairing the traditional with the nontraditional brings attention to both pieces," explains designer Vickee Byrum of this classic dining table mixed with modern chairs.*

CRAFTSMAN TOUCHES

T HIS AWARD-WINNING ATLANTA, GEORGIA, HOME WAS restored to its 1909 glory days but also renovated to be better. The kitchen is filled with craftsman touches, including hand-crafted glass-front cabinetry designed by one of the homeowners. The design eliminates cabinet hide-and-seek by allowing cooks to find a particular dish or serving piece with ease. Though the cabinets recall yesteryear, the owners opted for modern appliances—note the stainless-steel stove and restaurant-grade sink and faucet.

The seating is simple. It can be difficult to get a table for two at busy downtown Atlanta restaurants, but these owners have one that's always available and conveniently located at the end of their newly renovated kitchen. Covered in whimsical cloth that's easily changed out seasonally, this table serves as a place for meals and a handy drop zone for mail and keys.

Cheryl Kees Clendenon, of
In Detail Kitchen and Bath, on designing the Southern kitchen

I always find people want to be able to entertain in a comfortable, casual way. In the South, holidays and other rites of passage are celebrated in a big way, so the kitchen also has to be a gathering area for friends and families. If it's a small room, I'll incorporate banquette seating because it's an economical use of space, or I'll put a secondary oven or extra sink in a pantry or laundry room. In the South, you'll also find more open storage and cupboards for books and collections, so people can see the items they love and that express their personality. We're also seeing more wood countertops because wood brings warmth without formality. The kitchen has become command central. We're using single-level islands because if it's one big slab, you can fold laundry, do homework, and serve hors d'oeuvre there. And I'll incorporate at least a chalkboard on the inside of a cabinet, so women can keep track of family activities. I don't usually put in a desk, because, after all, what busy mom has time to sit down anyway?

RIGHT: *These owners show off some of their collections: piles of colorful dishes, figurines, and antique creamers. The cool collections are mingled with new additions like the Kitchen Aid mixer.*

FAR RIGHT: *Craftsman-style architecture, evident throughout the home, was the impetus behind this kitchen design.*

LEFT: *A collection of colorful dinnerware adds interest to the clean lines of the architecture.*

ABOVE: *The recipe for a great kitchen? A little ingenuity, a touch of whimsy, and a dash of craftsman style.*

LETTER PERFECT

I F YOU'VE VACATIONED AT ROSEMARY BEACH, FLORIDA, OR the surrounding area, then you're probably familiar with the Gourd Garden Courtyard Shop, which sells a creative mixture of wares including clay cookware, candles, hand-woven baskets, glazed pottery, tiles, and vintage glassware. Oh, and of course they also sell gourds galore from all around the world. A visit promises a new discovery on every shelf and in every corner. Shop owner Randy

Harrelson's Seaside, Florida, home provides much the same experience. It is filled with eclectic treasures of all shapes and sizes. The home is a journey, and along the path you'll find something new around every turn. The space is small, so incorporating storage solutions was important. For example, fabric covers the sink surround, and S-hooks display a collection of colorful cups. The eclectic mix is letter perfect from floor to ceiling.

ABOVE: *Like many of us, this homeowner just can't part with favorite treasures, so he displays them, adding personality to the small space.*

RIGHT: *This Seaside, Florida, kitchen takes advantage of creative storage solutions wherever possible.*

COOL AND COLLECTED

Elvis may have left one building, but he certainly found his way into another. This pool house/cabana is a collector's dream. It sports all manner of Elvis paraphernalia, including plates, pictures, records, and even a life-size Elvis cutout. The designers wanted to give the room a period feel. For example, "the curved bar is perfect for entertaining and provides a nice retro touch" says Angie Thompson of Pineapple House design firm. She notes, "We also wanted the space to feel like a lounge." Instead of building a single dining area, the designers incorporated several smaller seating areas to provide places for friends and family to visit in intimate groupings.

Even if you're not an Elvis fan—but what true Southerner doesn't love the king of rock-and-roll?—you're sure to glean some design tips from this cool cabana.

LEFT: *The homeowners, in the record business themselves, do a good bit of client entertaining in here. Across from the kitchen, a seating area with comfortable chairs and small groupings of tables allows guests to comfortably sit and talk or simply enjoy the show, whether a capella singing or karaoke.*

ABOVE: *If it's Elvis you're searching for, there's no need to look any farther than this Atlanta, Georgia, home. The rules for display? There aren't any. Just have fun decorating with the things you love.*

GET READY, GET SET

SOME MAY CONSIDER SETTING A GRACIOUS TABLE A CHORE, but Southerners relish the ritual. Placing the silverware just so, creasing the napkins, designing the place cards, crafting the centerpiece, coordinating the colors, and selecting the perfect menu drive many of us to a wonderful distraction. Dinner at a properly set Southern table is like a play where the set is as important as the actors. Whether we're planning for a romantic dinner for two, an intimate gathering of friends, or an all-out soirée, we go to great lengths to create stellar settings. Here, the owners of Atmosphere in Birmingham, Alabama, share their delightful designs and offer great take-home tips.

ABOVE: *Need a quick focal point? Group ceramic pieces of varied heights and colors. Tuck in fresh flowers and twigs or fresh fruits and vegetables.*

RIGHT: *Instead of a high centerpiece or traditional table runner, shells and candles are alternated. At one end of the table, vases are grouped to provide a point of interest.*

MORE TERRIFIC TABLES

THERE ARE NO RULES TO SETTING A STELLAR TABLE. DON'T be afraid to think outside the box. Go with what moves you, be it a dish, a color, or a theme. Try sheers or fabrics as tablecloths, or keep your surface simple by leaving the wood or other surface uncovered. Display a conversation starter such as a place card, a picture, or a piece of memorabilia. And, of course, don't forget the food. Use the recipes scattered throughout this book to inspire your inner chef.

ABOVE: *The table is decorated in natural tones of brown and tan and punctuated with pretty pink napkins for a pop of color.*

Setting the Southern Table on the Fly

Embrace the season. Look to your garden or yard to fill your table arrangements with nature's brilliance—try fall foliage, spring and summer blossoms, and winter bounty.

Display your treasures. Collectibles add interest to any table; vibrant ceramic pieces, pretty potted orchids, figurines, colored glass bottles, and well-cleaned sea treasures are just a few items to try.

Use serving pieces and dishes in unusual ways. For example, float flowers in a series of clear glass cups or bowls, or turn a basket or bowl into a silverware server.

WEST PALM RETREAT

Perhaps no state is more representative of eclectic Southern style than Florida, which reflects a mix of many peoples and cultures. Appropriately, this West Palm Beach retreat, designed by Pineapple House, is a coming together of styles and cultures that blend and mix and weave and finally merge into a cohesive look. Color is the bridge that unites these styles.

Slipcovers that might look fussy in the modern space look fresh when edged with bright blue trim. Window treatments, too, form a new design when edged with blue fabric. Modern lights that hang in an almost wavelike form grace the space above one of the tables, and blue accessories lighten the look throughout.

ABOVE: *White sheer slipcovers over the dining chairs keep the mood light and contrast with the heavy table, bookcase, and buffet in this informal dining area.*

RIGHT: *The crisp whites and blues of Florida's coastal waters as well as those of faraway Greece inspired the color palette of this South Florida home. "The room is enlarged when color blocks of blue and white are echoed in the artwork flanking its entrance," says Cynthia Peraso of Pineapple House. She explains that each seat back is sewn into a unique grid of white, cobalt, and chartreuse, and the designer added an acid-green glass disk to the center of the blue pendant chandelier.*

MODERN

ONCE UPON A TIME, THE SOUTH WAS KNOWN AS A rural region, filled with secluded country cottages shaded by wild woods and blooming vines. Many of us have since discovered wilds of a different kind, abandoning country roads and simple lives for paved city streets and high-rises. Instead of twinkling stars, city lights illuminate the night, and the hum of vehicles, not crickets, sings us to sleep. Urban expansion means loft living, cool condos, and modern style, and our interiors reflect that style with geometric shapes and chrome, stainless-steel, and lacquered finishes. To recapture the rural mood, we look to incorporate the outdoors with our interiors. We live and work and play in the city, but at the end of the day, we long for a serene escape. The clean lines and sophisticated modern style of the homes featured in this section epitomize this urban lifestyle.

This dining room is built for the comfortable modernist. It's not too stark, not too cluttered, but just right. "The chandelier is a rectangular steel pan that supports pillar candles," says Cynthia Peraso of Pineapple House. "Every candle is hollowed out, wired for electricity, and accepts a small, low-watt blub. The fixture is on a dimmer, so the mood of the room is easily modulated."

EASY BEING GREEN

THIS HOUSE MAY NOT HAVE A GREEN HUE, BUT REST ASSURED this Austin, Texas, house is green through and through. In fact, take one step inside the home and you feel better almost at once. Homeowner Sherry Matthews and architect Dick Clark collaborated on building this house to be environmentally friendly without sacrificing style. "In no way were design or aesthetics sacrificed to go green....My home has won many design awards and been selected for American Institute of Architects tours, and it always draws ahhs when people walk into it for the first time," says Sherry.

She explains, "My entire life I was plagued with allergies, taking allergy shots every week for thirty years...so I was diligent in researching products for my new home, seeing it as an opportunity to improve my health and to create an environment that at the very least would not make matters worse." Too, the green design fit right in with Sherry's work for an advocacy marketing group in Austin that runs campaigns for recycling and clean water. Her house is proof positive that she practices what she preaches.

And the story has a happy ending. After living in her house for nearly six years, Sherry says she no longer needs allergy shots and has tested negative to many things she was allergic to before. "I am the healthiest I have been in my life. My home feels clean and safe, and it is," says Sherry.

"In no way were design or aesthetics sacrificed to go green . . ."

—homeowner, Sherry Matthews

Dick Clark on the environmentally sensitive home

For me, green architecture is just common sense architecture. It's about dealing with the sun, wind, and weather. To start with, you can't design a house without first analyzing the site so you can maximize all those things that are free to use—the trees, sunlight, breezes. All the big windows in this house face east. In the morning, the owner opens them up and turns off the air conditioning. And this is the thing: If you've got them, you have to work with them. The next step is to make good choices like efficient HVAC systems, energy-saving appliances, low- or zero-VOC paints, and materials like concrete, which is inert because it's made with simple ingredients. For the floor, the owner found a farmer in Minnesota who harvests dead trees, brings them out of the woods with a horse, and mills them in his barn. But a lot of things that make building green are just common sense; they're hundred-year-old ideas, not ten-year-old ideas. Down here, houses have always had big sweeping overhangs and front porches. They weren't built as a place to put flowerpots but as a way to keep the wind and rain out.

RIGHT: *The dining room and kitchen are one large space, so entertaining is a breeze.*

ABOVE: *"My countertops are concrete, which I highly recommend because they are so wonderfully practical; I can set a hot pot anywhere and never worry about burning a surface!" says homeowner Sherry Matthews.*

RIGHT: *Sherry's green house provides a healthy and happy space for friends and family to share.*

Products in the House

Sherry shares a listing of products used in her home:

The flooring, certified from a sustainable forest, is white oak and finished in no-VOC wax. The planks are in varying widths, which increased the yield and resulted in less waste.

The cabinets are a special formaldehyde-free Baltic birch plywood.

The windows are thermal break, double-glazed, and commercial grade, with metal frames coated with long-lasting automotive factory paint. They open at both top and bottom for cross-ventilation.

Nontoxic paint and finishes were used for the walls and cabinetry.

LOFTY ASPIRATIONS

TALK ABOUT A ROOM WITH A VIEW! THIS LOFT HAS PLENTY OF them—both room and view. The open dining space and connecting living area were tastefully designed by Pineapple House to capture the vista of the twinkling Atlanta, Georgia, skyline. Look closely, and you can just make out the telltale IBM building.

Loft living is more popular than ever, and with the advent of New Urbanism, young and old alike are flocking to newly built downtown spaces and once abandoned but now revitalized industrial buildings. Instead of tearing down those delightful downtown buildings, loft owners are embracing the designs and delighting in character and details such as exposed beams, brick walls, and exposed ducts.

Many of the loft spaces are large. Plenty of square footage means owners need not sacrifice space to get the style they want. "In keeping with the industrial theme of this downtown loft, the custom oval dining table is made from concrete. It is surrounded by a midcentury, steel-colored banquette and contemporary upholstered gray side chairs," says Cynthia Peraso of Pineapple House Interiors. It's the perfect spot to enjoy the city scene without actually being in the midst of it.

ABOVE: *"The formal dining area is positioned in front of the two-story window in this enormous loft room, so guests can enjoy a spectacular view of the city while sharing a meal," says Cynthia Peraso of Pineapple House.*

RIGHT: *Dining in this room has a Jetson-like feel. The ever-growing Atlanta skyline warms the heart and soul. The interiors are arranged to take full advantage of the city views.*

FORM MEETS FUNCTION

WHILE WE APPRECIATE THE AESTHETICS OF STARK, NONFUNC-tioning spaces, because family and entertaining are so important, we understand that sleek and modern furniture that can't be sat on, slept on, or otherwise utilized is not viable. Luckily, Atlanta architect Bill Harrison of Harrison Design Associates understands that, too.

Meet one Atlanta family that puts the fun back in function. The modern, clean look of the home proves it is possible to have sleekness without giving up utility. Case in point: The two dining room tables can be pushed together or pulled apart as needed for game nights or intimate meals. Just for fun, people can change places during courses to mix things up. The colors of the space—cappuccino, cream, mahogany, and coffee—can be punctuated with bold and bright colors or softened with muted ones according to season or preference.

The same warm colors flow into the kitchen, where sleekly designed cabinets are easy to reach and filled to the brim with holding spaces for items large and small. Guests can perch on barstools to chat while the owners cook, and no one needs to make a coffee run with a coffee bar at hand.

LEFT: *Step right up to these sleek leather barstools. Their clean lines and padded seats provide both comfort and handsome design. Their light patterned color is meant to blend with the design of the nearby dining room.*

ABOVE: *Many families are choosing dining rooms with seating options. These square tables can be pulled together for formal family dining or left as a pair for more intimate gatherings.*

RIGHT: *This couple are coffee connoisseurs, so this mini-bar, with its small refrigerator and cappuccino machine, is perfect for them. The bar sink and handy storage facilitate morning coffee and late-night snacks.*

William Harrison on design for entertaining, Southern style

What we're starting to see is that the kitchen is now the entertainment space. People want the latest in appliances and high-quality materials in the kitchen because it's not just an area for cooking but also for hanging out, having a glass of wine. People are tremendously proud of their homes, and they like to show them off. We're also seeing more integration between the kitchen and dining area to create a better flow between the two spaces.

Often, people want an outdoor area with a patio and grill, especially in the South, because we have the luxury of using this area for most of the year. We're also getting more requests for warming drawers so food can be kept ready for whenever the mood of the party dictates dinner should be served and two dishwashers so everything will be clean and ready for service by morning. Even if it's only cocktails before going out to a restaurant, there's still a tremendous amount of entertaining in the home, with guests even participating in cooking, mixing drinks, and organizing appetizers—it's all part of the entertainment.

ABOVE: *Glass-front cabinetry breaks up what might otherwise be a stark storage wall. Elongated pulls offer a sleek, sophisticated look, and the blue-gray cabinets are offset by white marble countertops and backsplash.*

ARCHES DE TRIUMPH

SLEEK AND MODERN LINES CAN BE SOFTENED WITH A touch of Old World ambience. In the Old Enfield residence, for example, the design called for formal public entertaining spaces, but the kitchen and family room are far more modern. To ensure the two spaces flow as one, touches of classic styles offset the sleek space.

"The kitchen/family room…and the actual structure of the house is exposed, including steel and timber beams, metal air-conditioning ducts, and recycled vintage industrial lighting," explains the architect. "It is finished with recycled antique long-leaf pine that is more informal."

The kitchen cabinetry is from an Italian cabinetmaker and made in glass, aluminum, steel, and glossy enamel panels to contrast with the antique long-leaf pine. There is a traditional wood-fired pizza oven at one end and minimalist SubZero refrigerators, Wolf ovens, and a Thermador range at the other. Custom stainless-steel counters and sinks add to the look.

Going sleek and modern yourself? Here's the big reveal: The architects recommend contrasting old and new materials. "In this kitchen/family room, we collaborated with Austin artists such as Reggie Thomas, who created a painted glass panel that rolls back to reveal a wide-screen TV."

> *"The actual structure of the house is exposed,*
> *including steel and timber beams, metal air-conditioning ducts,*
> *and recycled vintage industrial lighting."*
> —Hobson Crow of Barnes Gromatzky Kosarek Architects

LEFT: *This kitchen is a mathematician's dream. Geometric shapes pervade the space. Half-moons, rectangles, squares, and circles can be found at almost every turn.*

RIGHT: *A gently arched ceiling leads the eye in and through the space to the cozy breakfast nook. The half-moon banquette offsets the straight lines used elsewhere in the kitchen while at the same time it echoes the ceiling arches.*

AN EYE FOR DESIGN

EVEN IF YOU'VE NEVER DONE ANY WOODWORKING, NEVER designed and created a piece of furniture, you will probably appreciate that creating such a work pairs brains with brawn. The clean lines of this white-on-white kitchen are reminiscent of a good furniture piece—one that is useful and utilitarian, with fine lines and function, comfort, and style. That's no accident, considering that homeowner and designer Laura Lee Samford not only plans interiors but also specializes in furniture design. The kitchen island is only one example of her handiwork.

"The island not only serves as counterspace and buffet but also the areas below are used for mixing bowls and cutting boards," explains Birmingham, Alabama, resident Laura Lee. Double sinks and a serious stove mean that she and her daughter, an aspiring chef, can cook side by side. "I designed this island," says Laura Lee. She explains that the piece is 10 feet by 5.5 feet (3 x 1.5 m) and is used largely as a buffet. Its oval top means it's often mistaken as a built-in kitchen table, which is fine with her.

Kitchen cabinets house all sorts of gadgets and gizmos. The cabinets were designed by Laura Lee based on an original by certified kitchen designer Cyndy Cantley. Glass-faced cabinetry mixes and mingles with closed fronts. To keep the clean look, Laura Lee built appliance garages into the kichen. All in all, the space has a clean, modern feel that does not lack in style.

Laura Lee on keeping it real

This house was built in 1951, and back then, especially in the South, it was not unusual to have a cook. The idea was that you were served. Kitchens were small, utilitarian, cramped, cut-up, closed-off spaces. This room was originally the laundry, kitchen, and butler's pantry. I removed all the walls and gutted the space. The island is the furniture in the center of the kitchen. In our previous house, our kids were teenagers, and they and our two big Labrador retrievers all wanted to be in the same space at the same time. We also entertain in the kitchen, so we wanted a lot of space. The top is one whole piece of marble, which is unusual, but you go into any Italian kitchen and you see marble. It's worn and stained, but it's wonderful. The beams are decorative, and they break up the volume of space. I also like the contrast of materials. I have white, I have stainless, I have rugged; it's mixing old and new in a European approach. Instead of making it look like a brand-new suburban kitchen, I wanted to create a space that looked like it evolved over time, which it has.

LEFT: *Now this is what we call island style. Instead of a square or rectangular island, this one was specially designed to have the appearance of a dining table. Like any traditional kitchen island, space underneath allows for convenient storage of utensils and cookware.*

*If you gravitate to a sleek modern feel,
it's important to strike a fine balance between style and sterility.*

LEFT: *Friends and family alike can gather in the kitchen to prepare large meals. Double sinks ensure that everyone who wants to can help with food prep.*

BELOW: *"We have two large Labrador dogs we love, and we wanted a kitchen that had plenty of room for the chaos that comes with them," says Laura Lee of the spacious kitchen.*

ABOVE: *This is the perfect place to park appliances. "The appliance garages provide a place for mixers and food processors that is very accessible but doesn't clutter countertops," says homeowner Laura Lee. Electrical outlets, she explains, are also housed in the garages.*

RIGHT: *Every kitchen needs a drop zone—a convenient place for a phone, mail (snail and electronic), cookbooks, and keys. This built-in cabinetry provides a spot to do just that.*

PART TWO
SOUTHERN STYLE FILE

P RESENTATION IS PRACTICALLY EVERYTHING. SOUTHERN AUTHOR JULIA REED wrote the following truism about Southern gatherings: "Southerners can't stand to eat alone. If we're going to cook a mess of greens, we want to eat them with a mess of people." Perhaps even more important than the perfectly prepared mess of greens, or grits, or sweet potatoes, is the certainty that they're served in true Southern style. That's why we Southerners take great pride in our kitchen and dining spaces and the products that we use.

Our kitchens and dining spaces are as varied as our landscapes, and they are filled with products wrought by artisans and craftspeople that take pride in their work and the region in which they live. The fine china and flatware that dances over our finely crafted dining tables, the cups and saucers that peak and spill out of kitchen cupboards, line our sideboards, and adorn sitting rooms are particularly chosen and often handcrafted and finely tuned to the spirit of our region.

In this product section, you'll find everything from rugs fashioned after South Alabama quilters to hand-painted pottery and woven table mats made from southern cotton. You'll find smaller companies and some big name brands that call our region home. No matter if you prefer punched pie tins or sleek sophistication, you're sure to find a product here to reflect the style you're searching for.

TRADITIONAL

Potpourri may be a classic element of every Southern dining room or kitchen, but this Cinnamon Cider Flared Glass Candle by **Aromatique** offers the same effect with a more elegant look.

Pull up one of these traditional barstools by North Carolina–based **Lexington Furniture**.

The subtle color palette and refined surface texture of tile ceramics by **Shaw Industries** pair beauty and durability. Pattern mosaics are repeated on the floor and fireplace, drawing the eye deeper into the room's inviting atmosphere.

Silver is a Southern staple. This three-section Swizzle Tray from **Mariposa**, maker of casual and elegant tableware, is literally a twist on the traditional—just look at that unexpected lip!

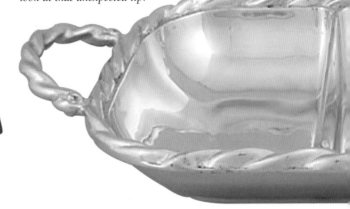

Wisteria *knows that summer nights in the South are made for drinking mint juleps from authentic cups like these. Don't forget the matching ice bucket.*

Cooking and entertaining are bound to lead to spills. Luckily, **Sunbrella**, *long-time maker of exterior weatherproof fabrics, makes beautiful interior weaves as well.*

Traditional Southern homes are rich with interior detail such as paneling and molding. Enliven your kitchen or dining space with **Southern Pine** *paneling painted in bold colors. For additional distinction, add painted molding to the ceiling and pair with bold patterned wallpaper.*

CASUAL

The folks at **Wisteria** call this country armoire "a big presence with a light touch." Available in a soft gray celadon, linen curtains behind screened doors hide a multitude of sins.

The wingback chair is a Southern staple. This Savannah Wing Chair from Atlanta's **Storehouse** is a variation on the more traditional wingback. Tropical detailing and cotton duck cushions make it the perfect addition to any home.

If you bottled the scent of the South, it would smell like freshly picked gardenias. **Aromatique**, of Heber Springs, Arkansas, has captured that essence with this delightful scented compote. Place it in the dining room or kitchen for a lasting Southern perfume.

These Rose Garden canisters by **Williamsburg Marketplace** were developed from a colorful appliquéd quilt in the Colonial Williamsburg historic collection. Its lovely pinks and greens will enrich the ambience of any space.

Get the casual comfort of an old farmhouse table with this new Momma Gina worktable from Atlanta-based **Storehouse.** Folding leaves allow the table to be used as a work or dining surface, and two built-in drawers allow for storage underneath. Match the table with a Bruno bench and two side chairs, and choose a celadon green base for a funky farmhouse kick.

Outfit your outdoor kitchen with appliances from Southern-based **Viking**, whose myriad appliance selections mean you don't have to spend time and energy mixing and matching brands and styles. That translates to more time spent actually enjoying your outdoor spaces.

RUSTIC

At just over 4 feet, this beautiful tray is made for serious work. Rich red and handpainted, the floral motif by **Wisteria** is reproduced from an antique piece.

This eight-lamp chandelier by **Shades of Light** adds drama and glow to any home. Place it over a dinner table for a vivid effect or to provide a rustic focal point.

Hadley Pottery is a specialty pottery stop in Kentucky that's renowned around the South for beautiful work. This casserole bean pot is handsome as a collector's item and useful as well.

In this flooring by **Shaw Industries**, soft variations in texture and color are combined with the unsurpassed quality and durability of porcelain to produce a rustic stone visual that enhances the décor.

This barley twist gateleg table from **Wisteria** will look good in your country home or your mountain cabin. Table legs swing out to support drop leaves. The piece seats eight with the leaves open and folds to a handsome display table.

No one knows how to do the holidays quite like the South. Capture the scent of the season year round with these candles from Southern company **Aromatique**. The brilliant red candles pop against their rustic wrought-iron holders.

Flooring, countertops, and cabinets by **Southern Pine** are guaranteed to add a warm and rustic touch.

ECLECTIC

A beachcomber's dream—shells that never break. These hand-crafted wooden shells with chipped paint and worn edges by **Wisteria** are the perfect addition to any seaside buffet.

We Southerners pride ourselves on our décor as much as our food. So, take famous Southern chef Emeril's kitchen advice into the dining room and "kick it up a notch." These plush chairs by Texas artist **Sallie Trout** are sure to be a topic at your dinner table.

Adjustable track lighting by **Shades of Light** comes in colors and styles as fun and funky as you like.

The folks at Atlanta-based **Storehouse** suggest that this utilitarian table works just as well for family game night as it does for casual gatherings of dinner and drinks.

No Southern dining room is complete without a service piece. This server is shown in the color shrimp to match our Gulf Coast cuisine. It's available with optional wine rack shelving and four adjustable shelves. Crescent moon handles add a funky finishing touch. Available through their Charleston show-room, **Maine Cottage** Charleston, South Carolina.

Modern

This monocottura ceramic by **Shaw Industries** *features a stone texture in three modular sizes that complements any décor.*

Holding onto a piece of furniture for sentimental value? Update a treasured hand-me-down chest or dresser with a fresh coat of paint and fun and funky pulls like these by Austin designer **Sallie Trout**.

For those who gravitate toward a modern look, Atlanta-based **Storehouse** *offers this simple, clean-lined table. It's the perfect combination of modernity and elegance in a piece that's simply Southern.*

Geometric shapes such as rectangles, squares, and circles fit right in with Southern modern-style urban spaces. This Cinnamon Cider Square Candle Jar from Southern-based **Aromatique** suits perfectly.

These modern chairs from **Ethan Allen** are sure to dress up your Southern setting, whether you're going for a modern or an eclectic look.

While a comfortable rocking chair has its place, the Southern modernist craves something a bit more up to date. This chair by Austin designer **Sallie Trout** fits the bill.

No Southern tablesetting would be complete without fine linens. Add a modern twist to your next design with this tablecloth from **Wisteria**.

Antenora Architects LLP
200 East Live Oak
Austin, TX 78704
P 512.462.1848
www.antenora-archs.com

Atmosphere Home Essentials
224 29th Street South
Birmingham, AL 35233
P 205.324.9687

Barnes Gromatzky Kosarek Architects
1508 West 5th Street
Suite 200
Austin, TX 78703
P 512.476.7133
F 512.478.2624
www.bgkarchitects.com

Vickee Byrum, Owner
Yellow Door Design
P 512.423.5230
F 512.482.8010
www.yellowdoordesign.com

Kathy Camp, Inc.
Contact: Juli Olson
111 North Marietta Parkway NE
Marietta, GA 30060
P 770.429.0970

Dick Clark Architecture AIA
207 West 4th Street
Austin, TX 78701
P 512.472.4980
www.dcarch.com

Cyndy Cantley
Cantley & Company
2829 2nd Avenue S # 120
Birmingham, AL 35233
P 205.324.2400
www.pepperplace.com

Ryan Gainey
129 Emerson Avenue
Decatur, GA 30030
www.ryangainey.com

Harrison Design Associates
3198 Cains Hill Place NW
Suite 200
Atlanta, GA 30305
William (Bill) Harrison, AIA; Robbie Pich
P 404.365.7760
www.harrisondesignassociates.com

Trip Hoffman
Designer and Real Estate Broker
810 Eisenhower Drive
Key West, FL 33040
P 305.294.3575

Bill Ingram, Architect
2205 7th Avenue S
Birmingham, AL 35233
P 205.324.5599

J.K. King Associates
347 East Conestoga Road
Wayne, PA 19087
P 610.896.4859

Luttrell Architectural Woodworks
607 North 31st Street
Birmingham, AL 35203
P 205.324.3421
F 205.324.3432

Sherry Matthews Advocacy Marketing
200 South Congress Avenue
Austin, TX 78704
P 512.478.4397
F 512.478.4878
www.sherrymatthews.com

Don B. McDonald Architect
117 West Mistletoe Avenue
San Antonio, TX 78212
P 210.735.9722
F 210.735.0366

Mary Evelyn Interiors
2910 Linden Avenue, 107
Homewood, AL 35209
P 205.879.7544

Cheryl Kees Clendenon
In Detail Kitchen and Bath
801 A North 9th Ave
Pensacola, Fl 32501
850.437.0636

Payette
285 Summer Street
Boston, MA 02210-1522
P 617.895.1002
www.payette.com

Pineapple House Interior Design, Inc.
190 Ottley Drive NE
Atlanta, GA 30324
P 404.897.5551
www.pineapplehouse.com

Frank B. Randolph
1671 34th Street NW
Washington, DC 20007
P 202.944.2120

The Rhett House Inn
1009 Craven Street
Beaufort, SC 29902
P 843.524.9030
F 843.524.1310
Reservations: 888.480.9530
www.rhetthouseinn.com

Laura Lee Samford
Interior Designer and Furniture Designer
2980 Cherokee Road
Birmingham, AL 35223
P 205.871.8712

Southeastern Construction and Management, Inc.
3198 Cains Hill Place NW
Suite 200
Atlanta, GA 30305
P 404.365.7757
Contact: George Cooke

Sallie Trout
Sallie Trout Designer
P 512-894-0774
strout@flash.net
www.troutstudios.com

Aromatique
PO Box 6000
3421 Highway 25B North
Herber Springs, AR 72543
P 501.362.7511
F 501.362.5361
info@aromatique.com
www.aromatique.com

Ballard Designs
5568 West Chester Road
West Chester, OH 45069
P 800.536.7551
Customer Service:
P 800.536.7551
F 800.989.4510
www.ballarddesigns.com

Bevolo Gas and Electric Lights, Inc.
521 Conti Street
New Orleans, LA 70130
P 504.522.9485
GasLights@Bevolo.com

Carpets of Dalton
3010 North Dug Gap Road
Dalton, GA 30722
P 800-262-3132
info@carpetsofdalton.com

Churchill Weavers
PO Box 39
Berea, KY 40403
P 859.986.3127
giftshop@churchillweavers.com
www.churchillweavers.com

Drexel Heritage
4240 Furniture Avenue
Jamestown, NC 27282
www.drexelheritage.com

Ethan Allen
PO Box 1966
Danbury, CT 06813-1966
P 888.EAHELP1
F 203.743.8298
www.ethanallen.com

The Furniture Company
7330 Market St.
Wilmington, NC 28411
P 910.681.0650
www.thefurniturecompany.net

The Gourd Garden Courtyard Shop
P.O. Box 611310
66 Main Street
Rosemary Beach, FL 32461
P 850.534.0070
F 850.534.0775

Hadley Pottery
1570 Story Avenue
Louisville, KY 40206
P 502.584.2171
F 502.589.0565
www.hadleypottery.com

Lexington Furniture
3024 Blake James Drive
Lexington, KY 40509
P 859.254.5362
www.lexington.com

Maine Cottage
Mailing address: PO Box 935,
Yarmouth, ME 04096

Maine Cottage store:
106 Lafayette Street
Lower Falls Landing
Yarmouth, ME 04096

Maine Cottage store:
525 King Street
Charleston, SC 29403
P 843.722.7188
www.mainecottage.com
Customer Service:
P 888.859.5522
F 207.846.0602

Mariposa
www.mariposa-gift.com
info@mariposa-gift.com
P 800.788.1304

Milestone Architectural Ornaments
4225 NE 9th Avenue
Amarillo, TX 79107
www.milestoneltd.com

Modern Design Expo
High Point, NC
P 336.510.2347
F 866.839.3154
www.moderndesignexpo.com

Norwalk - The Furniture Idea
Village at Mayfaire
Wilmington, NC
P 910.256.7919
www.norwalkfurniture.com

Shades of Light
4924 West Broad Street
Richmond, VA 23230
P 804.288.3235
P 800.262.6612
www.shades-of-light.com
visitor@shades-of-light.com

Shaw Industries
www.shawfloors.com

Southern Decor
2430 Teaster Crossing
Pigeon Forge, TN 37863
P 865.774.6732
sales@thesoutherndecor.com

Southern Living At HOME
P.O. Box 830951
Birmingham, AL 35283
www.southernlivingathome.com

Southern Pine
www.southernpine.com

Stickley Furniture
225 North Elm St
High Point, NC 27262
P 336.887.1336

Storehouse
P 888.STOREHOUSE
www.storehouse.com

Summer Classics
P.O. Box 390
7000 Highway 25
Montevallo, AL 35115
P 205.987.3100
F 205.987.3150
www.summerclassics.com

Sunbrella
P 336.227.6211
sunbrella.com

Thomasville
4257 Furniture Avenue
Jamestown, NC 27282
P 336.882.2100
www.thomasville.com

Viking Range Corporation
111 Front Street
Greenwood, MS 38930
P 662.455.1200
www.vikingrange.com

Wellborn Cabinet, Inc.
P.O. Box 1210
Ashland, AL 36251
P 800.336.8040
www.wellborn.com

Williamsburg Marketplace
P 800.414.6291
marketplace@cwf.org
www.williamsburgmarketplace.com

Wisteria
151 Regal Row, Suite 203
Dallas, TX 75247
P 800.767.5490
www.wisteria.com

PHOTOGRAPHER CREDITS

Paul Bardagjy/Through the Lens Management, 5; 6; 7 (bottom); 24; 25; 57; 58; 59; 116; 119; 120; 121; 128; 129

Emily Followill/Courtesy of Pineapple House Interior Design, Inc., 117

Tria Giovan, 12; 19; 26; 28; 29; 30; 31; 40; 41; 42; 43; 65; 66; 67; 68; 69; 77; 106; 107; 130; 132; 133; 134; 135

Steve Gross and Susan Daley, 20; 21; 22; 23; 78; 79; 80; 81; 82; 83; 85; 86; 87; 88; 90; 91; 92; 93

Mitch Hager/Courtesy of Harrison Design Associates, 32; 33

Jonathan Harper/Courtesy of Harrison Design Associates, 124; 125; 126; 127

Greg Hursley/Through the Lens Management, 16; 44; 52; 53

Sylvia Martin, 76; 94; 95; 110; 111; 112; 113

Scott Moore/Courtesy of Pineapple House Interior Design, Inc., 10; 11; 108; 122; 123

Daniel Newcomb/Courtesy of Pineapple House Interior Design, Inc., 97; 114; 115

John Umberger/Courtesy of Harrison Design Associates, 18; 34; 35; 36; 37; 38; 39; 70; 71; 72; 73; 74; 75

Brian Vanden Brink, 7 (top); 102; 103; 104; 105

Brian Vanden Brink/J. K. Kling Associates, 9; 13

Brian Vanden Brink/Payette, 54; 55

Deborah Whitlaw Llewellyn, 14; 15; 44; 60; 61; 62; 63; 109; 136

Scot Zimmerman, 46; 47; 48; 49; 50; 51; 96; 98; 99; 100

Photograph by Sylvia Martin

A LICIA K. CLAVELL IS EDITOR OF **Birmingham Home & Garden** magazine and former co-editor of *Southern Living House Plans* magazine, *Southern Living Kitchens*, and *Southern Living Bath Book*. She has also appeared as a design expert on Turner South's weekly program *Southern Living Step-by-Step*. Her writing has been featured in publications including *Coastal Living*, *Decorating Step-by-Step*, and *Southern Living* magazine.

ACKNOWLEDGMENTS

MANY THANKS TO THE HOMEOWNERS, DESIGNERS, AND ARCHITECTS WHO WELCOMED US INTO THE HEART OF their homes—their kitchen and dining spaces. Thanks to the photographers who captured these beautiful images with an eye for design and beauty. Appreciation to Candice Janco, Betsy Gammons, and all the other folks at Quarry Books for their tireless efforts in helping this book come together. To my parents, for making the decision to move to these sweet and varied Southern states. To Lynn Nesmith, who was ultimately responsible for this and so many other opportunities in my life. And, finally, special thanks to Ashley Arthur, David Ehrler, Bo McGuire, and Marli Guzzetta for their support to make this book a reality.